sunrise to sunset

P O E M S

Deborah Kenner-Sanchez

authorHOUSE®

AuthorHouse™
1663 Liberty Drive
Bloomington, IN 47403
www.authorhouse.com
Phone: 1 (800) 839-8640

Published by AuthorHouse 11/14/2017

ISBN: 978-1-5462-1432-8 (sc)
ISBN: 978-1-5462-1431-1 (e)

Contents

In loving memory of **Koda McKay Johnson**,
"Our Perfect Little Angel"

Acknowledgements

To my friend, Debbie Miller for editing,
To my niece, Krista Kenner for clerical organization,
To my husband, Arnie Sanchez for his patience and love,
And to my friends and family for their support and encouragement.

"Our Perfect Little Angel"

In loving memory of Koda McKay Johnson, my great-great nephew.

You were so loved even before your arrival.
But God had other plans for your survival.
He only takes angels in Heaven above
And fills their hearts with peace, joy and love.
He didn't want you to suffer or feel any pain.
Truly, our loss is Heaven's gain.
Our loved ones in Heaven will take great care
Of our precious little "Koda Bear".
So, goodbye for now our perfect little man
Until we can hold you in Heaven again.

American Pride

In loving memory of my father, Charles V. Kenner, U.S. Army, WWII

I am proud of the country in which I live
And thankful for all military and the service they give.
I am grateful and humbled by all veterans before
That sacrificed their lives in times of war.
They fought for our country and the right to be free
To give us the gift of our liberty.
The strength of a nation comes from the people within
That stand up for freedom and the country they're in.
Recognize all veterans, have them stand up tall
For keeping the dream....of life and liberty for all.

Everlasting Legacy

What will my everlasting legacy be?
I wonder what people will say about me.
Will they say she was clever, funny and smart?
Caring and sociable with a really big heart.
Or will they say she was crabby, stubborn and cruel
Along with being a big blubbering fool.
I want all to know about the love in my heart
And how each in my life played a significant part.
When thinking of me with a smile and a grin,
I wish kind thoughts and much happiness within.
I hope to be remembered for the stepping stones I've laid
And not for the wrongs and the mistakes I have made.

Friends

I have no money, yet I possess great wealth.
In good times and bad times, in sickness and health.
Love shared among friends is as good as gold.
For it cannot be bought, borrowed or sold.
Money means nothing if you don't have a friend,
That sticks by your side until the very end.
Wealth is not measured by money alone.
But rather by the friends, you call your own.

Lasting Impression

I met you once in a brief intercession.
You left upon me, a lasting impression.
That face, so hopeful and so kind
Still frequently lingers in my mind.
The words you uttered were so incredibly wise
That shown like a beacon in your heartwarming eyes.
A broken soul you have helped to mend.
For this, my gratitude, I humbly send.

Simple Pleasures

The simplest pleasures in life can be found
By opening your eyes and looking around.
We need not wealth nor golden treasures
To thoroughly enjoy life's simple pleasures.
Laugh out loud, simply giggle and smile.
Go see a friend you haven't seen in a while.
Take time out and thoroughly reflect
On the kindness you've shown and its lasting effect.
Give kisses and hugs on a daily basis.
These actions of love, time never erases.
Always give praise for the smallest of acts.
It gives others worth, a well proven fact.
Be thankful for life and make sure you address
The kindness of others and the love they express.
Always remember, the simplest pleasures can be found
By opening your eyes and simply looking around.

Laughter

All people laugh so differently.
Some people may chuckle or just go hehe.
Others may snort or even giggle.
Many may have their whole body jiggle.
Some laugh so hard they start to cry,
And may not remember the reason why.
Others may laugh till their bellies are sore,
Holding their stomachs and laughing some more.
When they're laughing so hard and doing a dance,
You know they're about to pee their pants.
Laughter, itself can be very contagious,
Especially when laughing about something outrageous.
So, remember to laugh at least once a day
And may deep in your heart this laughter stay.

What Is Love?

Love is an emotion that lies deep in our soul.
It makes our lives wonderful, happy and whole.
Love is a feeling that all people share,
Revealing to others how much they care.
Love can be instant or take time to grow.
It is given to others by the actions we show.
Love is patient, unselfish and kind.
It's putting others first and yourself behind.
Love is an act of great kindness and caring.
It's a part of our lives that is always worth sharing.
Love is eternal residing deep in our hearts,
Even though, from loved ones, we may be apart.
Love shown to God is the grandest of all,
Filling our soul when God comes to call.
So give your love freely, each and every day.
For tomorrow is not promised, but there's always today.

The Journey

Today you become husband and wife.
To share in the unknown journey of life.
Look at the journey, you have traveled to date.
To find your true love and forever soul mate.
The journey now shared may be bumpy ahead.
Not alone you will travel, but together instead.
Travel your journey with respect and trust.
Honesty and love are also a must.
Through good times, bad times, tears and smiles,
We wish you safe travel with many more miles.

The Road Less Traveled

The journey may take much longer
By taking the road less traveled.
Life lessons may become stronger
When the road is unpaved and graveled.
You learn from all the detours you take
And the bumps in the road ahead.
All the final decisions you make
Can give you new paths to tread.
So, be very bold and choose
A road that you never knew.
Because you simply have nothing to lose
By taking a different avenue.

Think Twice

When I was a child, I played games with my dad.
I didn't know then, I would one day be glad.
The games we played taught me to think and analyze.
My father was smart and incredibly wise.
Playing Master Mind, Monopoly and also Clue
Strategizing and planning about what to do.
Backgammon and Checkers, analyzing the next play.
"Think before you move" is what he would say.
Winning was not given, it had to be earned.
My thinking was challenged and life lessons were learned.
His legacy has given me an everlasting provision.
Always think twice before making any decision.

Decisions

Decisions are made every day
And a few may be hard to make.
The hard decisions we tend to delay,
Not wanting to make a mistake.
Some may be made instantly
And others may take more time.
Each should be made consistently
Cause they will last your entire lifetime.
Each decision is a success
And not a failure for you.
Because you have made an intelligent guess,
Learning from mistakes you accrue.

Hope

What has happened to our society?
This turmoil and chaos should not be.
We ask ourselves the question why
A person acts so others may die.
We often answer, "They are mentally ill."
Perhaps, that is why they choose to kill.
What lurks inside this troubled mind,
That they should hate all mankind?
Bullying, harassment, self-worth and more,
Are these the reasons we choose to ignore?
Real answers we may never attain
As to why a person simply goes insane.
We can only hope to embrace and enthrall
That kindness and love be given to all.

Wisdom

In loving memory of my mother, Wilma Jean Kenner

My mother did not finish her education.
But wisdom she had about every situation.
Her wisdom came from experiences in life
Through trials, tribulations and much strife.
Only as I age, do I truly appreciate
All the wise advice she had to relate.
I miss her dearly and wish she were here
To listen to me and lend me her ear.
So do not dismiss what a parent might say
Because you may need this wisdom one day!

Blind Date

This true love story is how I met my man.
I'll tell this tale as accurately as I can.
To a haunted corn field my family went.
These scary places, I do not frequent.
While standing in line for a rather long while,
They met a nice man who had a beautiful smile.
After leaving the corn field and exiting the gate,
They asked if he'd consider going on a blind date.
Scratching his head, he didn't know what to say.
But he gave them his phone number anyway.
My niece then gave his number to me.
She said, "He's attractive, just wait and see."
I debated and waited, then made the phone call.
It was either the beginning or the end of it all.
We went out for dinner, then went to a bar.
And what he said next was rather bizarre.
"I must show you something," he quietly said.
He took off his cap revealing his bald head.
"Women don't like men who have lost some hair."
I replied, "Right here and now, let's clear the air."
With a grin and a chuckle and in complete control,
"I'm not pulling up my shirt and showing my fat roll."
From that moment on and right out of the gate,
He knew that he found his forever soul mate.
For this blind date, I have my niece to blame
For changing my life and of course my last name!!!

Blue

When entering the house, we heard a loud sound.
A few items were overturned and scattered around.
What could have caused all of this mess?
A rather big mouse would be our guess.
I picked up the items and left for the store.
My husband had laid down to nap and to snore.
When I returned, he quickly jumped out of bed.
"We have not a mouse, but a squirrel instead!"
For a bit of advice, we called a dear friend
To ask what suggestions he would recommend.
Peanut butter was used and a live trap was set.
After a few tries, our goal was then met.
"We must let him go, it's the right thing to do."
My hubby agreed after spray painting him blue.
"Why?" I asked after he was all done.
"Cause if he comes back, we'll know he's the same one."

Lost

Directionally challenged, my husband might be.
East or west, left and right, he has trouble to see.
North or south, he doesn't know which way to go.
When reading a map, he is often quite slow.
In a wide open box, I'm sure he couldn't find
An easy way out of any kind.
He is very confident about one thing, I guess.
He knows how to program his GPS.
Without me as a guide and a wonderful wife,
I'm sure he would be totally lost in this life!!!!

Monday Night at the Fair

If you live in Upper, then you just might
Know Monday night at the fair is called "Hockemeyer Night."
It was named for two brothers from a long time ago.
Because, Monday was the only time they would go.
On Monday night you can enter for free.
Cause the fair doesn't start until Tuesday you see.
When telling my husband and explaining this tale.
Each year he recalls it with one missing detail.
He doesn't call the night the name it should be.
"Oscar Mayer Night" is when admission is free!

No Grocery List

I sent my husband to the grocery store
To buy a few items, just three or four.
After a while, I expected a phone call.
Cause there's always an item, he can't find at all.
I sent him for sauce, hamburger and spaghetti.
Wouldn't you think he would be back already?
When he arrived after a half-hour or more,
He didn't have everything I had sent him for.
Many other groceries I see he had bought.
And about the three items, spaghetti he forgot!
I learned a good lesson and perhaps somewhat more.
Always send a list and no extra money to the store!

TV Dinner

My husband is not a cook or gourmet.
But he really tried to please me today.
He placed tv dinners on an oven tray
Then walked in the room and began to say,
"How many minutes should I put these in?"
"How long does it say?" I said with a grin.
Thirty minutes on both is what he read.
Then follow the directions is what I said.
"But for how many minutes should BOTH be in?"
I sat there dumb-founded, holding my chin.
"Just put them in and I will take them out."
He had not a clue, I had no doubt.

Boober

To a beach in Florida, we all did go
And one of us put on quite a show.
Listen and picture this in your mind.
For this little story is one of a kind.
We were playfully bodysurfing all day long.
The waves were high and so very strong.
I rode in a wave and then turned around
Started laughing so hard, I fell to the ground.
Standing there with one hand on her hip,
She had no idea her suit top had slipped.
I was laughing so hard, I could not even speak.
When I pointed to her, she let out a big shriek.
Slightly embarrassed, she rolled up her suit top.
Both of us were laughing and could not stop.
This true beach story was her first claim to fame
And is exactly how "boober" got her nickname!!!!!

Cleaning the Deck

While waiting for him to prime a sprayer
To clean a dirty deck, layer by layer,
I was twirling a broom, when I fell through.
I know this may seem peculiar to you.
But a board did break and down I did go.
I'm sure it was a quite a hilarious show.
Throwing down the sprayer and pacing the deck,
My brother was scared and frankly a wreck.
One leg was bent back and the other one through.
My brother was unsure about what he should do.
"Pull me out of here," I said with a grin.
"Get me out of this hole that I am wedged in."
He frantically tugged and pulled my leg out.
Nothing was broken, but I let out a big shout.
So if you don't want your leg to look like a wreck,
Don't twirl a broom while marching on a deck!!! !

Diet Plan

Today, I'm sticking to a diet plan.
I hope all week, if I can.
One day at a time is what they say.
So, I need to make it through today.
Only one hour after eating my lunch,
I'm already thinking.....on what can I munch?
Dinnertime seems so far away
But on this diet, I must stay.
I want to lose two pounds a week
To shape and form a new physique.
My shape will look like an hourglass.
When, I finally reduce this big fat @$$!
In the near future, I hope to be
A beautiful and gorgeous, brand-new me!

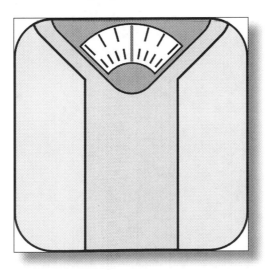

Melt Down

As you grow older, you lose some height.
Your skin gets saggy and not so tight.
I think in my case my height loss did trigger
The size of my feet, making them bigger.
Obviously, I am melting from head to toe.
I wonder how much bigger my feet will grow.
I need to lose weight so I'm not a plump ball.
Since, I'm losing some height and not very tall.
Diet and exercise will help lose this fat.
Before I disappear and go entirely flat!!

Pool Fool

A new friend of mine, I had met at school
Invited me over to her aunt's swimming pool.
"Just walk through the house, we'll all be out back."
But the woman inside had a near heart attack.
When looking at her, I felt like a fool.
"This isn't the house that has the swimming pool?"
"No, that's next door," she politely said.
"I'm sorry," I giggled, my face bright red.
I walked out of the house and entered next door.
I had never made such a mistake before.
The moral of this story should be clear to everyone.
Make sure the house you enter is always the right one!!!!

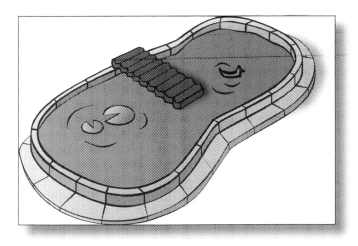

Pi Day (3.14)

Two geniuses share the same birthday.
Just who they are, I will not yet say.
I know this must be very hard to believe
And much more difficult to even conceive.
It could be fate or sheer destiny,
They share their birthday equally.
Both love mathematics and all permutations,
Solving the challenge of the right combinations.
They also share almost the same I.Q.
And love solving for variables in equations too.
There's just one more, little minor detail.
One is a female and the other a male.
Have you a clue, who they may be?
It's time to reveal this anonymity.
The first birthday belongs to Albert Einstein.
By now you have guessed, the second is mine!!!

Toilet Paper

You never know what you have until it's gone.
Especially when on the throne, you are sitting upon.
The tissue roll is empty, so what should you do?
You look and the Kleenex is even empty too!
You yell rather loudly and no one is there.
Maybe they didn't hear you or just didn't care.
Since no one answers, you are on your own.
Then suddenly the door opens and a roll is thrown.
You are so thankful, they heard your desperate plea.
But mostly you are thankful cause you only had to pee!

Valentine Sweetie

Today is the day you tell your sweetheart
How much of your life he has played a part.
It is a day set aside for you to reveal
The unconditional love for him that you feel.
You may buy flowers or a dinner for two
But the most special gift for him is you.

Autumn

Pumpkins, gourds, and bales of hay,
The cool crisp air at the end of the day,
Raking leaves in one large pile,
Then jumping in them after a while,
Such pretty colors, so vibrant and bold.
Autumn is a gorgeous sight to behold.
All too soon the trees will be bare.
And a freezing chill will fill the air.
All seasons are beautiful in their own way.
But, I so wish autumn was here to stay.

Witches Brew

Ghosts, vampires and goblins galore
Mummies, demons, bats and more...
This sight we see as we gaze down the street
On the night of Halloween's trick-or-treat.
All will be wanting candy, it's true.
Maybe we should serve them witches' brew!
Starting with water in a black iron pot,
This devious recipe, I haven't forgot.
Eye of the newt, toe of the frog
And don't forget tongue of the dog.
Curing and stirring, watching it boil....
Adding a few drops of lizard oil.
Blend in the body of a black widow spider...
This recipe makes a delicious spiced cider.
Serve this brew to see if they'll come back
For this scary Halloween trick-or-treat snack!

Feast of Thanksgiving

On the Mayflower, they sailed across the sea.
For the pilgrims wanted to be religiously free.
They sailed for Virginia, but went somewhat off course.
Because of strong winds and their powerful force.
Before arriving on land to unload and unpack,
They made new laws called the Mayflower Compact.
On a rock in Cape Cod, a few stepped ashore
To look over the land and briefly explore.
In a chilly November in the year sixteen twenty.
All pilgrims stepped foot on their new land of plenty.
To start their colony when winter was near
Would not have been wise at that time of year.
So, they built a few shelters trying hard to survive.
But, more than half of the pilgrims did not stay alive.
In the spring, they would build their Plymouth Colony
Diligently working to fulfill their prophecy.
They befriended two Indians who meant them no harm.
Who taught them to trap and how to crop farm.
By fall, the pilgrims were thriving at best.
Praising God for how much they had been blessed.
To celebrate their hard work and much success
And alleviate some turmoil and distress,
They prepared a large feast to feed one and all,
Which was called Thanksgiving, the feast in the fall.

Passe

Do you remember back in the day?
When the following inventions were not passe?
A black and white television set
With only three channels that you could get,
Heating all the leftovers on the stovetop
Instead of nuking and setting the timer to stop,
A transistor radio, that we so loved to play
And listening to the top hits of the day,
An LP or 45 spinning around
Hearing some scratches in the background,
Playing all the 8-track tapes we could find
Hoping the tape would not break or unwind,
Then a new version of a super 8-track
That was called a cassette with a front and a back.
We now have a disc which is called a CD,
That will soon be replaced by a USB.
Each new invention gets replaced someday
And will sooner or later become passe.

Masquerade

Attention and glory is what you seem to need.
But do you really need this to succeed?
It is not about having a notable name
Or the recognition and the glorious fame.
It is about who you are deep inside
And the actions to others that are bona fide.
Take off your mask, open your eyes to see
Inside your heart, how it really should be.

Missing You

I am sending you this little note
With no fancy, famous or written quote.
Because, I just wanted to briefly say
That I am really missing you today.

Moments

Moments in time may slip away
And we tend to forget sometimes to say,
Those three little words that mean so much
Followed by a gentle and loving touch.
Express your feelings, say them out loud.
Whether you're all alone or in a crowd.
A simple, I love you can make someone's day.
Don't let that moment in time slip away.
The past is gone and the present is here.
Whisper right now, "I love you, my dear."

Yesterday

I thought about you yesterday.
Remembering when, we would run and play.
We had no worries at that young age,
And playgrounds were our outdoor stage.
The first school dances we would attend
And passing those notes, we would send.
Learning to drive and getting the car.
Parents not letting us drive too far!
Then, seniors we were, in our last year,
And graduation day would soon be here.
In time, our lives would be re-arranged.
Forever and always, our lives would be changed.
Careers and families would be our goal.
Fate and destiny would take its toll.
Through the many years, some still survive.
Others have passed, no longer alive.
But our fond memories won't be swept away,
Because, I thought of you just yesterday.

Drifting Thoughts

Daily, my thoughts may drift of you
As I sit all alone in a daze.
I have no idea about what to do.
I'm living in a dense, foggy haze.
I miss you so much my dear
Each and every day.
I truly wish you were here
To take all my heartache away.
I know you are in a better place
Without any suffering ahead.
But, this doesn't fill the empty space
Or stop the drifting thoughts in my head.

Seasons of Life

Life imitates each changing season.
Perhaps, God meant this for a reason.
Spring signifies the season of birth.
The moment we arrive here on earth.
The season of summer may represent
Our daily lives and how they were spent.
In autumn, we are near life's last stage.
Whether we're young or in our old age.
In the bitter cold winter, our lives do cease.
It is at this time, we will rest in peace.
Life is renewed again in the spring.
When brand new life, the season will bring.

Passed

When you were a child, you invariably knew
Your parents would always be there for you.
Now as an adult, your thoughts have since changed
When life as you knew it would be re-arranged.
One parent would pass and then the other.
First your father, followed by your mother.
Memories that were made would always live on.
Even though your original family was gone.
This experience gives a new perspective on life,
To focus on happiness, not turmoil or strife.
And to live each day as if it were your last
Because one day, it will be you that has passed.

Celebration

In loving memory of my cousin, Thomas Jennings Frederick

Today, we celebrate your rebirth.
Remembering the time, you spent on this earth.
God has chosen to end your turmoil and strife
And bestow upon you, everlasting life.
We will miss you dearly, this is true.
But when chosen by God, we were happy for you.
As we reminiscence about the times we shared,
We remember your kindness and how much you cared.
Your heart was so full of peace, love and joy.
These qualities you owned, no one could destroy.
Standing here, before you today,
I can hear him whisper and lovingly say,
"Extend my love to all friends and family
For today and tomorrow have no guarantee.
So, begin the celebration of my rebirth,
Remembering the happy times I spent on this earth."

Sleepless

Another sleepless night
When sleep puts up a fight.
I can't shut off my mind
And leave my thoughts behind.
I toss and turn in bed
While thoughts go through my head.
I wish that I could sleep
But awake I seem to keep.
So again, I'm going to try
To get in bed and lie........AWAKE!

Genuine

Always be yourself, not phony or fake.
Because if you don't it would be a mistake.
If you try to be what you are not,
You will certainly be lost and often forgot.
Stay true to yourself, be caring and kind.
Treasure these qualities you have refined.
Open your heart and let others see
An honestly genuine personality.

Children of My Own

I hope I have touched the lives of many
Because children of my own, I haven't any.
My students have meant the world to me
And I count them as part of my family.
I tried to guide them in the right direction
With caution, care and loving affection.
I was always there to lend them an ear.
Not always saying, what they wanted to hear.
I have been honored to be a part of each life
And to stand by their side through happiness or strife.
They have touched my heart in ways unknown
And I will always count them as my own.

Wings

When a beautiful butterfly you may see,
Lovingly and fondly think of me.
I never will be truly gone
When on your shoulder, I may land upon.
For, I am flying in the heavenly sky
Upon the wings of a butterfly.

Life

I celebrate life as it is today.
It's not even a special holiday.
I woke up early and looked outside.
Standing there, I nearly cried.
How beautiful his creations are,
From a blade of grass to a shining star.
Life is a gift God chooses to give.
It's our choice how we choose to live.
Be kind and unselfish, giving to all.
No matter how tiny, minute or small.
Don't take for granted all things you see
And embrace each day most happily.
Each day is precious, not promised to you.
For today is a blessing and tomorrow is too!

The Football Game of Life

Life is like a football game
With continuous play by play.
Each single play is not the same
But unique in its own way.
We have to catch the tosses
In order to obtain,
Not highly significant losses
But precise and measurable gains.
Tackles, fumbles and penalties
Are obstacles that may take a toll.
We should huddle and try new strategies
To aid in achieving our goal.
We may not always be able to score
Or even win the game.
But giving one hundred percent or more
Leaves no regrets or shame.

Impossible Dreams

Always strive to do your best.
Take pride in what you do.
Don't take the path of all the rest
If it doesn't seem right for you.
Believe in yourself and you will achieve
Anything you set out to do.
All you have to do is believe
Impossible dreams can come true.

KODA BEAR

FOUNDATION

Established in the memory of Koda McKay Johnson

The purpose of the foundation is to comfort grieving families after the loss of a child. "Koda Bears" were created to give support to these families. Each bear contains a special message of comfort for the grieving family. The bears are then donated to hospitals, but are also available for purchase or sponsorship to other families.

All proceeds are donated to families who cannot afford headstones for their children. At the time of this writing, thirty-three stones have been sponsored.

Go to www.facebook.com/groups/kodabearfoundation.

Mission Statement:
"Let No Child's Resting Place Go Unmarked"

Printed in the United States
By Bookmasters